HOW TO BE A GOOD PRESIDENT

"Self-Help For The Confused"

Gwynneth Mary Lovas

ISBN: 978-0-9958170-6-7

This book is dedicated to Presidents the world over, who set aside ambitions for personal financial gain and social media popularity to devote their lives to the service of their countries.

Gwynneth Mary Lovas

TABLE OF CONTENTS

Gwynneth Mary Lovas

I. INTRODUCTION (AND EXPLANATION)

I am Mary Olsen, the President of Valhallaland, an ancient island nation originally inhabited by displaced Vikings, and which has been a democracy since the 17th century.

Of course you know who you are. You are the representatives of your nations, duly elected to the Office of President by the people of your nations through democratic process.

Congratulations on your Presidencies!

The question is, are you good Presidents, or are you confused?

As you are no doubt aware, there are hundreds of self-help books out there for people to read and study that provide all sorts of information on what to eat, how to lose weight, how to find love, how to achieve financial success, how to be successfully single, how to survive divorce and how to write an impressive resume. And these books can be of tremendous assistance for people in need of that kind of advice. But this is not one of those books.

This is a book specifically for you, my fellow Presidents, written by a President.

In much the same way that everyone who is not a President can find self-help books, fashion catalogues and personality and life-style quizzes in magazines to help them understand and better their personal behavior and appearance, this book was written with your personal betterment as a President in mind.

You see, contrary to popular belief, being a good President can't always be determined in advance by your lineage, your percentage of the popular vote, or even your rakish good looks.

It's also not easy to tell how good you are at being a President based only on the way your family, your nominees, hangers-on and those whose employment is dependent upon your goodwill treat you. Let's face it, our power to hand out big paychecks, employee perks, prestigious appointments, social and political connections and access to the seat of power make us pretty adorable to most family members, business acquaintances, potential nominees, would-be employees and hangers-on from the moment they first hear those words, "I do solemnly swear that I will faithfully execute the Office of President."

To say nothing of the impression we make on them the first time they see us sitting behind the big desk in the President's office, which only serves to make it virtually impossible for them to make any kind of accurate assessment regarding how good we actually are at being Presidents.

Some of us are even quite snappy dressers, which makes evaluating us even more difficult. Of course when I say "snappy dressers" I'm referring to suits, overcoats, shirts, blouses, scarves and ties - we are not trend-setting fashionistas, runway models or Yorkshire Terriers. But, while these accessories to our natural looks can make us more "good looking", even they aren't much of an indication as to whether or not we are technically good at being President.

The sad truth is, while we may all have the potential to be the most brilliant, productive, diplomatic, thoughtful, adroit, effective, circumspect and strong leaders on the world stage, I have personally witnessed and heard rumors (unfortunately supported by photographic and video evidence) suggesting that a few of you Presidents out there have lapsed into conduct unbecoming or detrimental to the dignity of your fellow Presidents. That's right, I'm talking about the excessive tweeting, nepotism, lying, lack of impulse control, leaking of classified information, incessant boasting and bottomless ignorance that are the hallmarks of certain Presidencies and end up being memorialized for all eternity on YouTube to the embarrassment of all Presidents past and present.

Every President deserves to know the truth. Certain behaviors are totally inappropriate for Presidents. And, while most of us over the age of majority will inherently sense when we are behaving and performing in ways that go entirely against the expectations of our advisors, our electorate, other members of the Executive, Legislative and Judicial branches of government, our Party, other world leaders and the media, there are those of us who just don't appear to be able to help ourselves, constantly crossing that line between appropriate Presidential behavior and engaging in activities that should really remain the domain of precocious children, notable and infamous people in the private sector, reality television stars, over-the-hill performers and others not accountable to the electorate or making use of public funds to support their activities.

My goal is to help all Presidents understand the true nature and purpose of the Office of President, and to encourage appropriate behavior that will demonstrate to the world where the line should be drawn between an obsession with social media and self-aggrandizement, and our dignity as representatives of the noble Office of President of our nations.

I have therefore taken it upon myself to write what is really a Presidents' self-help book, so that none of us ever again allow ourselves to succumb to weaknesses for inane expressions, outlandish hairstyles, preposterous lies, willful blindness, general pomposity and ludicrous facial expressions and hand gestures.

Every President deserves to know and understand how to be a good President, and to live up to the intended design of our respective founders, who went to a great deal of trouble and sacrifice to establish the democratically elected Office of President in our respective nations.

It helps if you think of it this way: the Office of President is one of the most precious assets, the crown jewel if you will, of your nation's democracy. It has existed long before you were elected to occupy it, and the people of your nation have every right to expect that, during your term, you will do nothing to tarnish it, mar it, bend it, break it, render it the subject of ridicule or detract in any way from its gravitas. Its significance goes far beyond your personal period of occupation. You are but a "tenant", and the landlord anticipates that you will turn over the property upon the expiration of your term in precisely the same condition in which you found it. Get it?

Let's just hope this advice isn't coming too late for any of you!

II. GENERAL CONDUCT

1. UNDERSTANDING THE JOB OF PRESIDENT

a. In General

Being a good President all starts with understanding the precise nature of your new job. While you might think this would be an obvious place to start, it's surprising how many Presidents are out there who ran for Office without understanding the nature of the position for which they were applying.

Surprisingly, the job of President of a country is nothing like being the CEO of a private sector business, or any other job for that matter.

In simple terms, because if you are reading this book you probably prefer me to keep it simple, a democratically elected President is usually the head of state and head of government of their nation, managing the Executive branch of the national government and acting as the commander-in-chief of the national armed forces.

You should also be aware, in general terms, that a democracy comprises four key elements: (a) a political system for choosing and replacing the government through free and fair elections; (b) the active participation of the citizens in politics; (c) the protection of the human rights of all citizens, and (d) a rule of law, in which the laws of the nation apply equally to all citizens.

For greater clarity, the rule of law is the legal principle that law should govern a nation, as opposed to the nation being governed by decisions of individual government officials. I get it - this can be a tough one to swallow when, after all, you are the most powerful person in the nation. It can seem counterproductive when you've gone to all the bother and expense of getting elected only to discover that you can't always do exactly what you feel like doing without checking first to make sure that what you want to do is "legal".

But trust me on this one, people living in democratic societies tend to be real sticklers about the whole rule of law thing, expecting the nation's laws to have influence and authority within their societies, particularly as a constraint upon behavior. And yes, including the behavior of government officials. I know. But it is what it is.

You see, a democracy contrasts with other forms of government where power is either held by an individual, as in an absolute monarchy or dictatorship (I agree, they do have a certain *je ne sais quoi* about them), or where power is held by a small number of individuals, as in an oligarchy, both of which tend to be frowned upon by people who have enjoyed the democratic experience.

b. Specific Powers, Duties and Functions

While every democratic nation will be unique in some respects, usually it is the Executive power of the nation that is vested in its President.

That power includes implementing and enforcing national-level laws, appointing your national government's Executive, diplomatic, regulatory and Judicial officers, and concluding treaties with foreign powers (sometimes subject to ratification by one of the Legislative bodies).

Presidents are often further empowered to grant national-level pardons and reprieves, and to convene and adjourn the unicameral or bicameral Legislature of their national government in some circumstances.

In many democracies, the President is also largely responsible for dictating the Legislative agenda of the party of which the President is a member. And, no kidding, you frequently enjoy a veto power! Cool, huh!

Finally, Presidents generally direct the foreign and domestic policies of their nations.

There you go. Done and done. Easy peasy.

c. Checks and Balances

As simple as all of that may seem, you should also be aware that virtually all democracies have been established relying on the political doctrine known as "separation of powers", which essentially provides for a constitutional government with three separate branches of government, being the Legislative, Executive and Judicial branches.

In short, the Legislative branch makes the law, the Executive branch executes the law and the Judicial branch interprets the law. And, it may surprise you to learn, each branch can have an effect on the other.

Each of the three branches is kept distinct in order to prevent something called "abuse of power", which is largely viewed by the people subject to them, as the major down side of absolute monarchies and dictatorships.

So, now that you get "why" democracies generally have a separation of powers, you probably are wondering how the powers of one branch can be challenged by another branch. Interesting stuff, no?

Well, that is what the system of checks and balances is all about, and it's probably worth having a general idea of the sorts of checks and balances common to most democracies - just in case you get confused by some of the stuff that your Legislative or Judicial branches might do.

Did you know that in many democracies the Legislative branch can, for example, impeach a President and conduct an impeachment trial, override a Presidential veto, declare war, approve national court system judges and enact taxes? Crazy, right? But certainly worth being aware of.

And if you think that's weird, "check" this out (pun intended) - normally, certain highly placed members of your Executive branch can actually vote that the President is unable to discharge his duties! You definitely want to keep that in mind - especially at Christmas - I'm just saying - a free round of golf at a swanky resort might not cut it.

Finally, in many democracies Executive (that's you) and Legislative actions may be subject to something called "Judicial Review", which is the power of the Judiciary to supervise the Legislative and Executive branches should they exceed their authority. Yes, it's true - your authority does have limits.

In simple terms, that's where a court can invalidate laws and decisions that they think are incompatible with a higher authority, such as a statute or the terms of a national Constitution.

So you want to be super careful when signing Executive Orders, as an example, that they don't contravene any national laws or the terms of your nation's Constitution. But don't worry, you will have lots of legal advice to make sure that you never get caught with your pants down, so to speak.

Which brings us to the next section. If you haven't been paying attention up to now, you should sit up straight, take notes if necessary and heed my advice very carefully. Even if you don't "get" what you have learned so far, if you follow the advice in the next section, that won't matter.

Nobody expects you to know everything. In fact, and I trust this won't come as a complete surprise to most of you, a large majority of people assume that you do not know everything.

I would even go so far as to suggest that there have been many Presidents out there whose intellectual horsepower has rested in neutral throughout their terms of office and that they, and their nations, have been none the worse off for it.

Why? Three reasons: (i) they had great advisors, (ii) they had the brains and the humility to understand how little they themselves actually knew, and (iii) they heeded the advice provided to them by the people who had the requisite levels of knowledge and experience to be providing advice in specialized areas.

2. CHOOSING ADVISORS

a. In General

Some Presidents who assume Office bring with them a wealth of education and experience. In short, these are the Presidents who are usually smart enough to know what they do not know.

Unfortunately, we have seen evidence that the pursuit of the Office of President of a nation can sometimes attract those individuals who aspire to power for the sake of power itself, and assume that they are suited to the Office because they actually do know everything and can do anything.

These individuals are called "megalomaniacs", an unflattering term because it includes the word "maniac", which rarely leaves a good taste in anyone's mouth, as it is commonly employed as a pejorative for individuals whose behavior appears reckless, or even crazy.

But, more than that, megalomania is actually a form of mental illness, which makes people believe that they have great or unlimited power. It is marked by feelings of personal omnipotence and grandeur, which don't tend to enhance one's abilities to work well with or listen to others.

It is actually quite easy to recognize megalomania. Megalomaniacs frequently refer to themselves and their achievements, insinuating their obsessions with themselves into almost any conversation, speech, meeting or interaction of any kind. Megalomaniacs don't even have the social grace to adopt false modesty. You will never hear false modesty come out of the mouth of a megalomaniac, which is one of the distinguishing features of megalomania, a mental illness, separating it from less serious personality traits such as over-confidence.

Watch closely for the use of superlatives. It is not simply the frequency with which megalomaniacs talk about themselves that is determinative, it is the always glowing and never negative terms with which they constantly describe themselves and their achievements that separates them from the rest of us. Sort of like narcissism, and frequently occurring in combination therewith, but more to do with power.

Conversely, they cannot help but describe their adversaries in extremely negative or poor terms. To sum up, while they will use terms like "great", "the best", "the most", "tremendous" and "successful" to describe themselves and their accomplishments, they will use words like "terrible", "horrible", "the worst", "disaster" and "nut job" to describe their adversaries and anything their adversaries have done or attempted to do. They will always assume credit for everything positive. They will never assume responsibility for anything negative.

The real problem with megalomaniacs achieving high office is that, far from being prudent or circumspect, exercising caution and forethought in the face of risk or danger, these people cannot be counted on to be prudent, watchful or discreet. They will make decisions and act without considering all of the circumstances, and they will ignore possible consequences.

Needless to say, these traits have the potential to be a total disaster and possibly dangerous in a President.

Assuming that you do not fall into the megalomaniac category, which you probably don't if you are even reading this self-help book (megalomaniacs notoriously don't believe they can benefit from anyone else's advice), then this is the most important section of this book for all President's who genuinely want to be good Presidents.

Understand and accept that you will need all kinds of advice in order to do your job well.

Forget about your cronies. Just because someone was a friend or associate in your private life does not qualify them to be a trusted advisor in your role as President. You will need to surround yourself with people who are specialists in and have proven track records in government, public administration, law, economics, environmental science, military strategy, counter intelligence, international affairs, industrial security, human rights, privacy, policy development and ethics, to name a few.

Forget what you think you know, what your "gut" tells you and what your life before politics taught you. They will be of almost no value whatsoever in your new role as President of your nation.

Find the most qualified advisors you can and make a point of seeking their advice.

If you have chosen well, your advisors will help steer

you through the complexities of your new position with ease and grace, and your nation will be a greater and safer place for it. You're welcome.

b. Nepotism

And this would be where we have to touch on one of the more sensitive subjects. No self-help book for Presidents would be complete without some discussion of nepotism which, as you know, is the practice of persons in positions of power or influence hiring relatives.

To be specific, outside of banana republics, dictatorships and absolute monarchies, nepotism is generally looked upon as both foolhardy and verboten.

The word is based on the Latin root, *nepos*, meaning "nephew", originating from the time when it was common practice among church officials who had no legitimate offspring of their own to give their nephews positions of preference, in much the same way that a father might give his son a job.

But you are not a medieval church official, you are the President of your nation, and subject to far more scrutiny.

And, tempting though it may be to look upon your offspring as being genetically superior to all other conceivable candidates for the position of advisor to the President, the chances of that actually being the case are almost guaranteed to be slim to none.

My advice, therefore, is to wish your children well in their respective careers, support them in their personal endeavors (so long as you do not create any conflicts of interest or appear to be endorsing their business activities in any way that might be contrary to public policy), and invite them for dinner occasionally like any good parent would.

You may even choose to slip them a few bucks every now and again, so long as the bucks don't come from the public coffers.

But do not, under any circumstances whatsoever, no matter how brilliant, attractive or nice you may sincerely believe them to be, open yourself or your children up to public scrutiny and ridicule by actually hiring them to assist you in any way, shape or form.

And, although it should go without saying, I will say it anyway. This advice extends to all of your relatives. Hiring relatives not only makes you look like a fool, it actually confirms that you are a fool. The love, respect, admiration, guilt or whatever else it is that you might feel for close relatives should never translate into giving them jobs paid for out of the public purse. Period.

The only case I can even think of where such a hiring was successful, is an American example from the 1960s but, sadly, very few of us have relatives the ilk of Robert F. Kennedy. Believe me (with apologies to my relatives, who are all brilliant, beautiful, talented, lovely people).

3. HEEDING ADVICE

Presumably by this point you can see the wisdom of my advice about choosing qualified advisors.

But here's the thing. You will derive almost no benefit whatsoever out of having made great choices for advisors if you do not then also do two very important things.

First, much as you might think you can rely on your own judgment, unless you are wondering what to eat for dinner, which tie to wear, chatting about the weather with your mother or discussing your children with your husband or wife, in pretty much every other set of circumstances during your term of office, you must seek the advice of your advisors.

Second, having taken that step, you must then follow the advice provided to you by your advisors, even when you are "almost positive" your opinion is just as valid. It isn't. Ever.

In sum, if you pay no attention at all to anything else in this self-help book, please do Presidents everywhere a huge favor and heed my advice about seeking and heeding advice. You will thank me, your nation will thank me, and history will thank me.

4. LANGUAGE AND TERMINOLOGY

a. Vocabulary

You have aspired to become the leader of your nation. You have succeeded. From this point forward, every single word that comes out of your mouth will be scrutinized, examined, studied, analyzed, dissected, debated, judged and recorded for posterity by people all over the world.

It is a very humbling experience the first time you wake up in the morning to find your words splashed across the front page of an important newspaper, or flashing across the screen of a national news program. You do not ever want those words to give the impression that you have poor judgment, that you are ill-advised, that you are a racist, a sexist, a narcissist or a dumb-ass. It is also a bad sign if even one editorial suggests that you should provide proof that you graduated from high-school.

This is why your language skills are extremely important. Remember, you are no longer speaking as a private person, you are the voice of the Office of the

President of your nation. Your words purportedly reflect the intelligence, policies, laws, ethics and values of your entire nation on the world stage. You are speaking as the voice of millions of people, many of whom obviously voted for you. Under no circumstances should your words do them harm or bring the integrity of your citizens into question.

That being the case, I can offer some simple tips to help you present the right image:

1. While it is acceptable to describe your nation, other nations, other individuals or the accomplishments of other individuals as "great", "brilliant" and "fantastic", it is rarely advisable to describe yourself or your own achievements as "great", "brilliant" and "fantastic". A little humility can go a long way. Leave it to history to come up with appropriate words to describe you, your achievements and your Presidency.

2. As useful as the word "great" can be, try to mix it up a bit to give the impression that you have at least a moderate command of the language. You don't have to be Winston Churchill, but maybe consider reading a few books or buying yourself a thesaurus. There are lots and lots of really good words out there. Try learning a few.

3. The more frequently you use a word, the less meaningful it will become and the less impact it will have. As an example, if every person you like, every meal you enjoy, every national accomplishment, every meeting that succeeds and every broadcaster who agrees with you are all described as "great", you come across as being not terribly discerning. Use the word

"great" to describe those few things that truly deserve to be described as "great".

4. Same goes for over-use of any superlatives, positive or negative. Everything you don't like or disagree with is actually not "horrible", "terrible" or a "total disaster". Try using some subtleties and nuance in your language choices. There are thousands of words out there, many with quite specific meanings that may be more appropriate to describe the people, events, undertakings, successes, failures and things which please and displease you, or truly represent your hopes and aspirations.

5. While people do appreciate it when you appear to be capable of relating to "the common man", your language skills should not be so common that you end up sounding like you are speaking down to people. There is actually a special word that captures my meaning precisely. It is "patronizing".

6. Neither do you want to come across as a simpleton, which strongly suggests that you represent a nation of simpletons because, after all, they did elect you. It is almost never appropriate for a President to publicly refer to any individual as "that guy". And, unless you are referring to a "citified" person visiting a rural location, it is never acceptable for a President to use the word "dude". It is slang. Simply saying, "I know words" isn't enough and, quite frankly, begs the question, "Then why aren't you using them?". If, indeed, you do "know words", you might wish to consider using more than a few

dozen of them. Even Koko the gorilla "knows" two thousand words.

7. Feel free to adopt the occasional multi-syllable word into your lexicon. Don't be afraid that people will think you are "too smart". While your citizens likely expect you to be capable of relating to the needs of the average Joe, they generally expect their President to be smarter than the average Joe.

8. You should have access to seasoned speech writers. Use them. Shooting from the hip can result in injuries.

9. Use honest, sincere language, appropriate to the message and the occasion. Say what you mean. Mean what you say. Otherwise your words have no meaning. You should never have to use the expression, "What I meant was..." Worse, your representatives should never have to use the expression, "What he (or she) meant was..." If people are continually feeling compelled to explain what you meant, either you are not making yourself clear, or you did mean what you said, but what you said was illegal or politically unpalatable.

10. Refrain from using repetitive, pat phrases. They can come back to haunt you. Believe me!

b. Technical Terms

The use of technical terminology deserves a category all its own.

Many words have quite specific meanings, but none more so than technical terminology. And, as it is incumbent upon a President to know, understand and employ technical terminology in appropriate circumstances, I have taken it upon myself to provide some minor assistance in this regard.

1.   McCarthyism: McCarthyism is broadly used to define the practice or policy of persons in authority making unproved allegations against innocent people without any regard for evidence. Just as an example, if a person in authority, without any evidence to substantiate the claim, publicly accuses another person of committing a high crime, say, for example, wiretapping their telephone conversations, then that would be McCarthyism. Let me be clear. The person making the claim against the other person is guilty of McCarthyism, not the other way around. So to say, "This is McCarthyism" following the unsubstantiated claim is, in fact, correct. Although why anyone guilty of McCarthyism would then feel the need to point out that they are guilty of McCarthyism is difficult to understand. Do I need to repeat myself? Okay: The unfounded public allegation of the high crime of wiretapping from the person in authority is McCarthyism. No need to follow up with the statement, "This is McCarthyism". The rest of us know it is, and have enough sense to know you should try to avoid it.

2.   Grandstanding: Another quite specific term generally accepted to mean seeking to attract applause and favorable attention. Pretty much synonymous with "showing off". It is a term frequently and accurately applied to persons who have notably sought the limelight most of their

lives, and tend to aggrandize themselves and their accomplishments in front of the media. Rarely appropriately used to describe persons who have lived a modest life of public service well into middle age and appear to be reluctant to discuss themselves or their "greatness" in front of the media.

3. That's Taken Off: An infrequently used technical term, the precise meaning of "that's taken off" is, to a large extent, dependent upon the words it follows. For example, following the words, "This sweater is super itchy", the words "that's taken off" are almost certainly meant to indicate that "I have removed the itchy sweater." Following the words, "I faced great pressure because of Russia", however, lends an entirely unique interpretation to the words "that's taken off". In that case, "that's taken off" has absolutely nothing to do with itchy sweaters, and is far more likely to mean, "I have removed the Russia pressure." I grant you that the grammar and sentence structure are poor in either case, but the meaning becomes quite clear when the subject matter to which the technical term refers is stated unambiguously.

4. Believe Me: "Believe me" is a technical term that is short for the statement, "You can put your complete trust in whatever it is that I am telling or promising you." Conventionally, it is a personal guaranty of the complete accuracy of what it is you have said or promised and should only ever be used when you are one hundred percent certain of what it is you have said or can absolutely guaranty the fulfillment of your

promise. That being the case, you may want to consider using it sparingly, and only in the circumstances in which I have described. Use of the term actually puts your trustworthiness, character and credibility on the line. Every time you use it. If, just as an example, what you are promising requires the agreement of another person whose agreement has yet to be secured, there is no rational basis upon which to use the term. Make that mistake just once, and it will come back to haunt you. In fact, the more frequently you use the term, the less likely you are to actually be believed. Almost no-one can guaranty the actions of third persons in advance of them having taken such actions. At best, the meaning of the term will then actually morph into something more like, "Please believe me" or "I want you to believe me", neither of which is even close to be being as effective or meaningful as, "You can put your complete trust in me." At worst, it ends up meaning something more along the lines of, "You can trust that I am going to bully everybody I can for as long as it takes to get what I want," which gives the distinct impression that you are either arrogant or stupid, and is just plain alarming. Especially these days, what with all the anti-bullying messages around. People don't seem to have the same fondness for bullying they once did.

I provide this advice because, for those of you who have difficulty using multi-syllable words and certain phrases, my hope is that you will risk using them now that you know how to use them appropriately and accurately. *Bonne chance!*

5. USE OF SOCIAL MEDIA

a. In General

First of all, you will want to think long and hard about even using social media.

As Presidents, we usually have at our disposal many other means of creating and sharing information, means that are not generally available to those for whom social media is the only outlet for expressing themselves. You have staff to keep the public informed about significant matters. There are press briefings, speeches, public appearances and many other more traditional means of letting your nation know what you are up to, what your plans are and what you think on virtually any topic worthy of discussion by a President.

While an occasional *bon mot* or insightful remark of a more personal nature may endear you to your electorate, you should at some point at least ask yourself whether or not it is really necessary or wise to have your every brain fart memorialized for all eternity on Twitter. Remember, you can't "unsay" stuff on Twitter. Sure, you can try to explain or leave your staff in the position of having to try to explain your words after the fact, but it is so much simpler if you refrain from tweeting ridiculous things in the first place.

And when I use the term "ridiculous" I don't mean merely "uncharitable", "questionable" or "somewhat inaccurate", I mean absurd, unreasonable and deserving of being held out as the subject of derision and mockery. As President, there are absolutely no circumstances in which you want to open yourself, your family, your government or your party to ridicule. If you are ridiculous, it strongly suggests that, at the very least, the people who voted for you are also ridiculous.

b. Specifics

Which brings me to more specific advice. In the event that, notwithstanding my advice to avoid personal social media accounts in general, you feel compelled to share your personal thoughts with "your public", there are some very serious rules that you really must consider following:

1. Under no circumstances should you twitter, tweet, text or share in any other way your personal thoughts on either matters before the court, or decisions made by a court of competent jurisdiction. You will recall at the beginning of this book where I mentioned that one of your duties as President is to uphold and enforce national laws? Govern yourself accordingly.

2. Threats, veiled or not, are absolutely prohibited. A threat from Bob who lives down the street doesn't have nearly the gravitas of a threat from the sitting President of a nation. If Bob tweets that you had "better hope" that he doesn't have a video of who keyed his car, you can take it with a grain of salt, especially if you didn't key his car. If a sitting President tweets that you had "better hope" that he didn't tape his conversation with you, it can only mean one of two things: (i) the sitting President has tapes of your conversation (which may or may not be a relief to you), or (ii) the sitting President wants you to think he has tapes which will contradict what he imagines you might say in the future about your conversations with him. Neither is less disturbing than the

other. In fact, both possible interpretations just make you come across as a weirdo, and both are highly inappropriate for a sitting President to state publicly.

3. Accusations of any sort on social media are to be strongly discouraged. False accusations may open you up to any number of tedious legal proceedings, and are rarely to your benefit. I refer you back to the section on McCarthyism for greater clarity on the matter.

4. Call it boasting, bragging, grandstanding or showboating, by any name self-aggrandizement is (i) entirely unnecessary (you have already won the election), (ii) childish, (iii) overtly defensive, (iv) smacks of narcissism or some other personality disorder and (v) serves no legitimate purpose. Hint: If you are as great as you think you are, other people will be the ones saying so. If you are the only one saying so, it means that you are actually not as great as you think you are. It's one thing to crave admiration from others; it is an entirely different thing to engage publicly in self-admiration. Yikes! If you're doing it, knock it off! Very unpresidential.

6. INTERACTIONS WITH OTHERS

a. Your Staff

As a President, you undoubtedly have staff.

Your staff are there to advise and support you, take the heat for you, prop you up, let the nation and the world know how brilliant, kind, thoughtful and diligent you are and generally stand by you.

Here's the crazy part. They actually expect you to do the same for them. I know. It's not like they are paying you! Wait a minute - yes they are - in fact, the entire population of your nation is paying you - good thing to keep in mind.

But that aside, the last thing you ever want to do is blame, undermine, contradict or throw your staff under the proverbial bus. At some point, one or two of them might object - perhaps even publicly. Having trouble with leaks? Try taking somebody out to lunch once in a while, why don't you. In short, if you don't make fools out of or blame your staff, they will do their utmost to cover for you when you make a fool out of yourself. Remember, the buck actually does stop with you, whether you know it or not.

b. World Leaders

This topic is more easily covered with a simple "what not to do" list:

1. Don't ever make the mistake of assuming you are more clever than other world leaders. One or two of them might surprise you.

2. Never allow yourself to be perceived as the toady of a foreign regime.

3. Don't make broad, sweeping statements about the personal characters of other world leaders. Those words may come back to bite you.

4. Don't assume everyone wants to be your friend, or that they are as taken with you as they pretend to be. Many of them have been schooled in something called "diplomacy". Have you never even heard the expression "hidden agenda"?

5.   Don't meet a foreign leader without (i) learning how to pronounce their name correctly, (ii) learning a little something about the country they represent and its history (size doesn't always matter), (iii) realizing you do not have to impress them - they generally know who you are, (iv) brushing up on your country's current and past relations with their country and (v) trying hard not to offend.

c. The Media

For starters, you might benefit from understanding the role of the media in modern culture.

Unless you have been living under a rock your entire life, you probably know this, but - just in case - generally, the media, which includes the press, broadcasters and publishers, are the means of mass communication of news and entertainment. If you do it right, your Presidency will be more the subject of news than entertainment.

In a larger sense, the media can actually help create and shape public opinion (very worthwhile keeping in mind), and are an essential element of any democracy. And, while national leaders in countries where the media is controlled by the government certainly have it easier than the rest of us, we should appreciate that, at their best, media outlets act as watchdogs to protect the public interest against malfeasance by creating public awareness and accountability. A "free press" provides a public check on government, sometimes referred to as The Fourth Estate, a term that has been around since the 18th century.

Not that I am advocating this, but if you are planning a coup, for example, the first thing you want to do is seize control of all media outlets and dictate what they print and broadcast. I know - sounds like fun - just not so much for your citizens.

But in the democratic world, we actually hold our media in high esteem and to high standards. If they print or broadcast slanderous, libelous or false stories, they can be sued. While you may not like what they say, or the way they say it, it is extremely rare for respected media to engage in "fake" news. It would, in simple terms, be costly and counterproductive.

Most media outlets refuse to print or broadcast information without a reliable source and corroboration from at least one other source. They also normally ask the subject of what they are about to report if they have anything they would like to say about the subject matter. Very much on the up and up.

All of that being the case, as with many human interactions, you can expect to find differences of opinion among media outlets. But those you treat with respect will generally accord you the same.

An attack on the media is an attack on democracy itself, so you never want to be disrespectful to members of the media. There is no democracy in which that is advisable or productive. You see, we aren't allowed to imprison our dissenters. You don't need to be a sycophant with the media, but you do need to understand the significance of media relations. You should be able to hire advisors to help you with this. Like your other advisors, they should know how to deal with the media appropriately. Take the advice your experts are paid to provide.

I find that openness, transparency and the truth are often productive stepping-stones to good media relations.

In addition, many Presidents recognize that the media is an effective tool in helping to spread, not just the democratic message, but your government's specific policy messages throughout the world. So my advice is to embrace the media as an essential arm of democracy and an important tool in helping your administration get its messages out.

d. Your Family

Bearing in mind my advice about nepotism, just a quick word about relations with family during your term of Office.

If your spouse isn't by your side during your term, people are going to assume that there is trouble in paradise. In nations built on family values, that is a negative message. Being the President is a tough job, and it is reassuring for people to believe that their President has the support of his or her family during the tough times. If you and your spouse can't commit to standing by each other during your term, where does that leave everybody else? That lack of mutual support says something. What it says is anybody's guess - and that's the problem - everybody will be guessing.

Finally, you don't want to demonstrate a marked preference for one of your children in public. It makes you look like a bad parent or weird. Treat all your children equally in public. It's the right thing to do.

e. Government Officials

While your personality should not lend itself to immediate and indiscriminate friendships, you should have sufficient self-confidence to stand your ground and meet overtures from other government officials without expressing hostility or appearing nervous or skittish.

Note: This is pretty much the same advice I would give to German Shepherd Dogs about their encounters with strangers. For some weird reason, it applies equally in this context.

f. Members of Another Sex/Sexual Orientation

Many countries today strongly encourage equal rights among the sexes, be they male, female or intersex which is, I assume you know, a "real" thing.

Members of all sexes expect to be treated equally and with respect. Essentially, there are only two "rules"

1. The minute you start behaving in an overtly sexual way towards another person in a public environment, people will assume you have yet to reach socio-sexual and/or emotional maturity. Not an optimum or Presidential impression.
2. Presumably your nation, much like the rest of the world, is made up of a combination of people of all different sexual orientations. I have three words for you. They all vote. And, as the person in charge of upholding the law, you do not want to start exhibiting biases for or against any sex or any sexual orientation, which is, in many countries, contrary to law.

7. INTEL

A priority of any government is to protect the safety, security and privacy of its citizens both at home and abroad.

The preservation of national security is usually a multi-faceted endeavor that requires cooperation across a diverse range of initiatives and programs, often with a specific body of national security advisors providing the Executive branch of government (yes, that's you) with national security and foreign policy advice and coordinating work in counter-terrorism, critical infrastructure, cyber security and transportation security, to name a few, among various national and international departments and organizations.

One important element of maintaining national security and protecting the safety, security and privacy of your citizens is the classification of information under the care and control of the government. That includes everything from personal information and confidential business information collected by the government, to information generated by the government itself (memoranda, correspondence, analyses, reports, etc.).

All government employees who originate or receive sensitive information in any format, including electronically, are required to mark it according to the level of protection or classification appropriate to the nature of the information.

Every piece of sensitive information must be marked, stored, communicated, shared, retained and destroyed in accordance with the highly specific requirements of the assigned level of protection or classification, whether "protected", "confidential", "secret", "top secret" or other.

In all cases, only individuals who have received the requisite level of security clearance and have a need to know the information may view the information. Meaning no-one who does not have a "top secret" security clearance as well as a need to know the "top secret" information is permitted to view or hear about any information classified as "top secret".

Information that is "classified" as opposed to merely "protected", if compromised, may cause injury to your national security. "Top secret" information is extremely sensitive classified information related to international affairs, law enforcement investigations and intelligence matters which, if it finds its way into the wrong hands, may cause exceptionally grave injury to national security and risk lives.

You don't ever want to be on the wrong end of an inadvertent release of "top secret" information to the wrong persons. And you most definitely do not want to be caught revealing "top secret" information "on purpose", "just to see", "because you were asked", "because you wanted to impress somebody" or "just for fun".

In fact, in many democracies, anyone who knowingly communicates classified information to an unauthorized person, or uses it for the benefit of any foreign government to the detriment of their own government may be liable to prosecution and possibly face a lengthy prison term.

Of course as President, the likelihood of you ever doing such an unthinkable thing is extremely slim, in light of the fact that you will be well briefed on all sensitive national security matters from day one, and will be the recipient of extensive advice in this regard.

All of which is to say, while you will get "great intel", you will also get "great advice" on how to protect that "great intel". I can't stress enough how important it is to actually follow that advice!

8. ETHICS

This is a fun topic, and one with which I'm sure most of you are familiar.

Your citizens will, quite rightfully, have every expectation that you will have a highly developed personal code of ethics by the time you become their President. In order to not disappoint in that regard, I will provide some truly basic information that will be of particular assistance to those of you who have been encumbered by significant private business interests prior to assuming office or have had to look up the meaning of the term "ethics" as it is generally understood.

Everyone wants to have a certain level of confidence in the integrity of their government, which is to say that nobody thinks your work in or for the government should benefit your personal financial, social or other interests or aspirations.

The greater your authority and influence (power), the more likely it is that you are in a position to positively affect your personal interests through what you know and do in your official capacity. Needless to say, a president is right up there at the top of potential for conflicts of interest. Your position as President will almost certainly offer the opportunity for you to further your private interests, or the interests of your relatives, friends or persons with whom you have been or expect to be affiliated.

Therefore, neither you, members of your family nor any individual, group or organization with which you have had or expect to have a connection should be on the receiving end of any financial or other benefit because of the information at your disposal or the decisions you make in your official capacity as President. Impartiality is a requirement of your decision-making authority.

This prohibition will also mean that you may have to divest yourself of certain property and interests prior to assuming office. Alternatively, you can separate yourself legally from those interests by ensuring that you have no influence or control over them.

But, not to worry. There are very likely laws and policies in place to help ensure that you have no conflicting financial interests and can make decisions impartially. Thank goodness for all those advisors you have. This can be a bit of a sticky wicket to try to figure out on your own, as the legal provisions can be quite technical (as legal provisions are so frequently wont to be).

One of the more common ways of resolving one type of potential conflict of interest is to establish something called a "blind trust" whereby, in exceedingly general terms, you turn over management of your problematic assets to an approved trustee.

I know it can feel excessive, but surely you must see how, just as an example, your access to non-public government information or property could potentially be used to serve your private interests. Wouldn't everybody love to have access to the kinds of information at your fingertips. Here's the thing. That information and property is paid for by and supposed to serve the public. I know - arguably a waste. Nonetheless, you are required to avoid conflicts of interest and remain impartial in the exercise of your official duties. And don't forget, nor are any Executive branch employees entitled to use their government positions to endorse any private sector products or people.

While all of this can take a bit of the fun out of being President, keep in mind that your citizens do need to have confidence in the integrity of their President. Not kidding.

9. PUBLIC SPEAKING

Here's where most Presidents shine, so I hardly have to provide any advice at all. If you have been elected to the Office of President of your country, then no one can question your talent for public speaking. That said, a few of us Presidents have noted the occasional instance of a less than talented public speaker being elected President.

Without naming names, let's just say that it has been known for a President to be elected, not so much because of their brilliant public speaking abilities as due to an unaccountable blip in voting habits or a wave of public sentiment or frustration that has, to everyone's surprise, including their own, resulted in them actually winning an election. So it is with that category of Presidents in mind that I offer this bit of advice.

What to do (Note: if you can tick off five out of eight from this list you will be doing very well):

1. Be sincere;
2. Be direct;
3. Demonstrate a real grasp of the issues at hand;
4. Use self-control;
5. Express yourself in clear terms;
6. Be respectful;
7. Avoid the use of superlatives, and
8. Be positive.

What not to do (Note: even getting one of these wrong will be problematic for your Presidency):

1. Outright lie;
2. Be less than truthful;
3. Deflect;
4. Leave the impression that you don't understand the complexity of the issue at hand;
5. Act pompous or be self-congratulatory;
6. Make rash statements;
7. Wing it, or
8. Be negative.

Remember, thrilling though it may have been to hear applause when you were running for office and making any number of outlandish promises, people have a tendency to pay even more attention to your speeches when you are speaking with the authority of the President and all that that entails.

Now is the time to be circumspect. If you have to look up the word "circumspect", your election probably falls into the "surprising results" category and you should memorize the above advice before opening your mouth again.

10. WISDOM

What is wisdom? Well, it is the quality of being wise, and for those of us occupying the Office of President, it is usually good enough if we can even give the impression of being wise.

There is little that brings more satisfaction to a President than to be widely reputed to be wise, to have everybody think that we house in our brains a body of knowledge and experience that we bring to our every decision or action. What confidence such a reputation would inspire.

And so, it is with that goal in mind that I offer these few humble suggestions:

1. Know many words;
2. Know what those words mean;
3. Use those words accurately;
4. Know facts;
5. Know the difference between fact and fiction;
6. Know science;
7. Listen;
8. Answer the question you are asked, not some other question you wish was asked;
9. Pay close attention to wise advisors, and
10. Use superlatives sparingly.

11. TRANSPARENCY

a. Government Transparency

Sure, people throw the word "transparency" around like they can lay claim to it any time they want just by saying it, and regardless of its applicability to them and to what they do.

They use the word because they know it "sounds" good. it sounds like the right way to go, the implication being that all your government's actions are scrupulous enough to bear the closest public scrutiny.

Here's the problem. As good as it may sound to claim transparency, it is quite another for a government to be completely open.

My advice? Steer clear of adopting the term at random. While it is possible to promise transparency for something like the awarding of lucrative government contracts, it is an empty and meaningless promise when it comes to government operations as a whole.

Government, by its very nature, can never be completely transparent in absolutely everything that it does. "Yep. We've compiled a list of all the suspected terrorists whose telephones we're tapping this month. Sure, I have a copy right here."

To name but a few, there will frequently be security, diplomacy, privacy and safety issues at stake that prevent governments from letting everybody have a hard line into all government computers and speakers broadcasting everything discussed at every government meeting.

Your actions and the actions of your government are not necessarily less scrupulous or ethical simply because you cannot make them all transparent. So don't pretend they are or even can be.

You are already required to comply with the laws of your nation, so your actions must, first and foremost, be "legal". That should not require your continual confirmation. If your actions are not legal, those "checks and balances" I talked about earlier will uncover illegal acts.

Further, you are already "accountable" to your citizens. If they don't like what you do, they can elect somebody else next time around. So touting your "accountability" is just as empty as feigning "transparency".

So let's find another word, a word that means honest and with integrity. Hey, here's a crazy idea. How about we just say that from now on. "This government undertakes to govern with honesty and integrity."

We can do that. It doesn't have to be an empty promise. Novel, true, but I think people might go for it. If we mean it.

b. Personal Transparency

I just know you're really going to love this part.

While it is true that government can never be completely transparent, you actually can be. Surprise! I know. It really is as simple as that.

What's more, not only "can" you be transparent, your country actually expects you to provide full disclosure of all your personal financial dealings in conformity with the historical practice of sitting Presidents.

It's a great and easy way to build trust and give your electorate confidence that your actions as their President will not violate conflict of interest laws and policies. Nothing says you intend to govern your nation in accordance with the highest ethical standards possible quite like releasing your tax returns!

This is where your openness and transparency can really count, and set the tone for your entire Presidency. And it's a great way to demonstrate your commitment to accountability. Congratulations!

12. IMPULSE CONTROL

Ever look at yourself in the mirror before going to bed at night and think, "Gosh, I wish I hadn't done that."

Ever wonder half-way through a speech, "What on earth possessed me to just promise that?"

Ever review the notes from a meeting and ask yourself, "Did I say that out loud?"

Ever peruse the newspaper headlines over breakfast and speculate, "Did one of the kids use my Twitter account again?"

Well, it's happened to the best of us. Call it getting caught up in the moment, misspeaking, being carried away or just plain forgetting where you were, it all boils down to the same thing, impulse control.

And the last thing you want is people thinking (or saying) that their President is "unstable". That will take the fun out of being President faster than the time it takes to move from one Netflix episode into the next.

So, I have come up with a solution to this thing that plagues all of us from time to time.

Of course there are the old tried and true methods of discipline and self-restraint, but they're not so easy to maintain when you've had a long day.

That's why my solution is a simple, two-pronged approach to curbing impulse control. I personally use it, and find it to be extremely effective:

1. Turn your mobile phone off at night, and
2. Wear an elastic band around your wrist. Every time you are about to open your mouth in public, just snap the elastic hard against your wrist. It really does tend to alter your focus, which, if you are prone to outlandish statements, is not a bad thing.

So give it a whirl. If you don't find yourself saying stupid things less often then I'll resign my job as President - oops - forgot to snap the elastic. Damn! Yep, self-inflicted wounds are the hardest to heal.

13. ENTERTAINING

A President is presumed to have learned normal social skills by the time he or she is elected to Office.

You were not elected to be "the life of the party". Your demeanor should never scream, "Whoopee! Hijinks!" when you step into a room.

You are never going to have, nor do you want to have, ten thousand friends on Facebook or followers on a personal Twitter account. Refer to my section on "Use of Social Media".

The very nature of your Office is also such that it makes it extremely unlikely that people will ever be inspired to salute you with a "chest bump" or a "high five" when you arrive on the scene.

These truths could be interpreted as the "down" side of being a President for those whose craving for attention and affection knows no bounds.

On the "plus" side, however, that same *gravitas* that is inextricably linked to your Office, and essentially precludes your nomination for the "Miss Congeniality" Award, will normally be of tremendous assistance in helping you perform whatever entertainment duties you have been assigned without having to worry about strangers trying to pull you in for an unwanted and unwarranted "hug". Yech. It's always so weird when strangers or mere acquaintances presume a level of familiarity that, in polite society, is reserved for family and close friends.

All of that aside, your duties as President will require you to entertain important people of every ilk, but more importantly, foreign dignitaries.

As President, you will have been provided with an Official Residence. In most countries that residence is not only historically important, but also of highly symbolic importance to your citizens and, in all likelihood, to the foreign dignitaries visiting your country. That is why it is customary to invite foreign dignitaries to that residence.

Nobody is really interested in being invited to your privately owned digs to be entertained, no matter how fancy. Foreign dignitaries are never going to proudly display photos of or advertise the fact that they had dinner at some "other" place, even if it is considered (along with thousands of other places or buildings like army bases and churches), to be a "landmark". Foreign dignitaries are not visiting your nation as tourists, they are coming at the invitation of the President. However great it may be as far as you are concerned, and however proud you may be of owning it, it will be of no symbolic significance whatsoever to a foreign dignitary.

Foreign dignitaries can and do get invited to countless castles, palaces, fancy estates, homes, clubs and restaurants. When you extend an invitation, they expect to be given the "full treatment", which means being entertained in the symbolic and historic Official Residence.

Anything less is insulting, and makes it seem like you are treating them like tourists and trying to impress them with your personal assets, which (i) are highly unlikely to actually impress foreign dignitaries, and (ii) mean absolutely nothing to anyone but you.

It also hints that you don't think your nation has provided suitable accommodations for receiving dignitaries or that you are trying to "outdo" your predecessors, both of which are just plain rude.

Remember, they have accepted an invitation from "the President" and not from you in your personal capacity. They don't give a darn about what you own in your personal capacity. They want to be entertained by "the President" and accorded the respect they are due as foreign leaders who have been invited by you to visit your nation. So, unless you plan on donating this "other" place to the people of your country, my advice is to stick with protocol.

14. GROOMING

A good President always sets a good example with his or her grooming.

Proper grooming includes:
a. Brushing your hair;
b. Brushing your teeth;
c. Cleaning the "eye-boogies" that collect in the corners of your eyes (as required);
d. Checking and cleaning your ears (as required);
e. Nail clipping (as required) and
f. Bathing/showering.

Presidents should be confident when it comes to their personal appearance. Remember this should anyone try to convince you that you would look great with a comb-over or should dye your hair an unnatural color. While it was at one point avant-garde for people to add a dash of blue, orange, purple or green to their hair, that has never been a good look for a President. Not even on Halloween. Seriously.

Finally, never mind what "all the other guys are wearing". You are a President, and owe it to yourself and to Presidents the world over to maintain a semblance of dignity that will go straight out the window the first time you even "wonder" how you'd look in a trucker cap. You are not a trucker. You are not a baseball player. You are a President. You can put one on temporarily for a fun photo-op to promote a special (preferably charitable or sporting) event, but that's it. It should never come to symbolize your Presidency. I mean really, how ridiculous would that be!

Which, of course, brings me to my next topic, self-awareness.

15. SELF-AWARENESS

Never mind what your family, your employees and the toadies who surround you tell you about yourself or your actions.

Never mind what you have believed of yourself since Mommy said you were "really cute", "really smart" or "really great".

Forget about the good press you get from your friends and how much support you get from people you have made promises to.

Real self-awareness comes from your critics.

I know. This is a bitch. But it's true. Your starting point towards real self-awareness should be what your worst critics say of you. Take it all in. Write it all down. Then force yourself to ask the tough question, "Is there some grain of truth to what is being said?"

Of course there will be critics who criticize simply for the sake of criticism. You will have encountered opponents, met people of different points of view and possibly even made enemies along the way. But just because an enemy is saying something doesn't make it not true.

In fact, an enemy will be the first to point out your most blatant errors or egregious traits. What your opponents say can often be startlingly accurate, because they will have honed in on your most obvious weaknesses from the start.

But in general, you can get a balanced viewpoint of yourself if you look to the source of the criticism. That should give you a good indication as to whether or not you have been unjustly vilified or accurately nailed.

Then look to the numbers of sources. If one source is saying something negative, you probably don't need to lose sleep over it, annoying though it may be. If one hundred sources are saying the same thing, you had better take a closer look in the mirror.

Learn from your critics. Unlike your staunchest supporters, they generally don't want anything from you. They will be the ones who will tend to tell it like it is. Sure, they may elaborate or take advantage, but if a number of sources are criticizing the same thing, think long and hard before you decide to label them all as liars or incompetents. Accept some of the responsibility for your reputation and focus that blinding spotlight on yourself.

If you seriously believe that an entire group of people are "out to get you" in an Orwellian conspiracy of biblical proportions, chances are you are actually suffering from something called "paranoia". That would be a problem for any President, particularly so for the President of a nation with nuclear capability. Why do you think nobody is booking a vacation to North Korea? Get a grip on yourself and on reality. Paranoia is frequently associated with a number of personality disorders, none of which are pretty.

Remember, your reputation is actually in your hands. Missteps can always be forgiven, and if you are very lucky, you may even have the opportunity to correct some of your less than perfect qualities. *Carpe diem.*

16. GETTING OVER YOURSELF

Yes, I have saved the best (and shortest) advice for last.

Get over yourself. You won. Everybody knows you won.

You don't have to announce it every time you meet somebody new. They know you are the President. That is why they are there to meet with you, see you or listen to you. Has anybody ever once said, "Really? The President? I did not know that!"

If you continue to act surprised that you are the President, people are going to start wondering whether or not you actually are the President.

Exception: For clarification purposes only, as when somebody walks up to the guy beside you and says, "Nice to meet you, Mr. President." Then, and only then, can you say, "I'm the President."

III. DEAR MADAM PRESIDENT

1. INTRODUCTION

Following are excerpts from my *Dear Madam President* advice column found at theretirementdiaries.com.

2. LETTERS

a. Prefect Pontius

Dear Madam President,

Apparently in my zealousness to demonstrate how powerful and decisive I am here in Judea, I've gone and executed a really great guy. A really popular guy. From what I understand, he may have been the Son of God. Now I'm trying to come up with a way for history to exonerate me and blame the crowd. Is this possible?

Sincerely,
Prefect Pontius

Dear Prefect Pontius,

First of all, my sympathies. I understand that this can be a very trying time for you. To say nothing of what eternity will be like if, indeed, you did execute the Son of God.

The whole "taking credit for the good and laying blame for the bad" is a very "un" prefect-like move that few can survive. However, if you have a great relationship with the media, you may be able to convince them to write a lot of fake stories about how you tried to convince the crowd to spare the Son of God but the crowd insisted on the execution. Only then is there any hope that history will be kinder to you than you deserve. And if you can get them to throw in a fake story about a symbolic gesture you performed for the crowd suggestive of you having washed your hands of the whole messy decision-making process, that might help lay the blame where it doesn't belong. Who knows. Only history will tell.

Good luck with that, and with the whole eternity thing. And remember for next time, it's always better to get your intel in advance of taking bold, irreversible steps.

b. Emperor Genghis

Dear Madam President,

I've recently put a lot of trust in my generals. I regard them as close advisors and have given them a fair amount of autonomy as far as dealing with other nations is concerned. They appear to have taken more initiative than I had bargained for and, while they do demonstrate the unwavering loyalty I require of them, I've heard rumors of large-scale subterfuge that may affect my popularity in lands I have conquered. I believe that even my tenure as Emperor may be at risk. It's a total disaster. At least that's what the civilians are saying. What do I do?

Sincerely,
Emperor Genghis

Dear Emperor Genghis,

Hmm. That is a poser. I do wish leaders would seek my advice prior to allowing these sorts of things to happen.

That said, something you need to understand about senior members of the military is that they are actually trained to be decision-makers. So when you give them that level of autonomy, they are going to go ahead and make decisions, some of which you might not agree with. A good rule of thumb is to establish some checks and balances within your administration to ensure that the big decisions go through an approval, or at least a consultation process first from now on. Fewer surprises that way.

As far as the fallout for what has already happened is concerned, if you can convince the civilians that your generals acted outside the scope of the authority you gave them, you might be alright. Alternatively, can you not come up with some way to silence them?

I can see your heart is in the right place. You just need to work on understanding human nature and controlling your administration. Maybe even listening to advice if you are lucky enough to get it in advance of the problems occurring.

Best of luck!

3. HOW TO CONTACT MADAM PRESIDENT FOR ADVICE

If you would like to have your request to Madam President for advice published online, please send your submission to madampresident@valhallaland.com.

You will be notified if your submission has been selected for publication.

IV. THE PRESIDENTS' SONG

Although it is recommended to be sung in groups of three or more, solo performances can also be quite inspiring, particularly when accompanied by an obliging pianist.

You are encouraged to invite your staff to join in the refrain.

Members of the media are permitted to observe.

THE PRESIDENTS' SONG
(Sung to the tune of "Jingle Bells")

I was elected just last week
And was told I must make sure
To not let information leak
If I'm to keep our land secure.

And so I read a lot of books
To make sure I knew the score
Learning new stuff is my job
So if you can please teach me more.

(Refrain)
Hey! Presidents, Presidents
We're smart as we can be
And we will protect our folks
From sea to shining sea.

Hey! Presidents, Presidents
We're loyal and we're true
But if you don't like us
You know precisely what to do.

For my meeting yesterday
My staff prepared me with some notes
Therefore I knew just what to say
To make sure we don't lose votes.

So when my day came to an end
And I turned on the T.V.
I tuned in to CNN
To make sure you still like me.

(Refrain)
Hey! Presidents, Presidents
We're smart as we can be
And we will protect our folks
From sea to shining sea.

Hey! Presidents, Presidents
We're loyal and we're true
But if you don't like us
You know precisely what to do.

V. A NOTE TO OUR ELECTORATES

If you have ever known a President, you probably know what happens from the moment the clock radio turns on in the morning.

Whether we have it set to talk-show banter or classical music, it doesn't matter. A President always hears *Reveille*. It is the President's equivalent of the Bat Signal. If our eyes are open, we are already at DEFCON 4.

Presidents are hard working people. In fact, no matter how busy we are, if you want us to do more, we will gladly assume greater responsibilities.

My point? Please let us know what it is that you would like us to do. We want to work. You can't ask too much of us. We need to keep busy, and we love a challenge. We can handle all the mental stimulation you can throw at us.

If you forget why you elected us, we will remind you. If you don't know about threats to our nation, we will alert you. If health care, job security, immigration and protecting the environment for future generations are on your mind, please bring it to our attention. In addition to undertaking any tasks that you ask of us, we learn from our experiences and can anticipate your needs before you are even aware of them.

If you support us in our endeavors to help our country and our citizens, we will devote all our energies and the resources of our nation to whatever you ask of us. We will stand beside you, we will listen to you, we will support you, and we will protect you and those you love to our last breath.

Our Presidencies are about fulfilling your dreams, not ours. We are Presidents, and that is what we do.

VI. PRESIDENTS' CODE OF CONDUCT

1. PREAMBLE

Whether you are new to your Presidency or a seasoned veteran, as a President you must represent all of the people of your nation who have entrusted you with the power and the resources to look after their best interests.

Your Code of Conduct is clear and uncompromising. Learn it. Live by it.

2. DUTIES AND RESPONSIBILITIES

A President shall, in accordance with the high degree of responsibility bestowed upon that Office, at all times fulfill all duties and responsibilities imposed by applicable law, serve their nation to the best of their abilities and protect all citizens against illegal acts.

Service to your nation includes assistance to those citizens who by reason of personal, economic, social or other emergencies are in need of immediate aid.

In the performance of their duties, Presidents shall respect and protect the dignity of all of their citizens and maintain and uphold the rights of all citizens.

Presidents may authorize the use force only in accordance with the law and only to the extent required for the performance of their duties.

No President may inflict, instigate or tolerate any unnecessary act of harm, cruelty or other degrading treatment or punishment on any person.

Presidents shall protect the health of their citizens and, in particular, shall take immediate action to secure appropriate medical services for their citizens as required.

Presidents shall respect the law and this Code of Conduct. They shall also, to the best of their capability, prevent and rigorously oppose any violations thereof in accordance with the provisions herein, including enforcement of punishments against other Presidents who are in contravention of this Code for first and second offences.

In the conduct of their services, all Presidents must:

a. Understand that their primary responsibility is to safeguard the lives and property of their citizens, prevent offences and preserve peace and order and

b. Remain faithful in their allegiance to their citizens and strive to attain excellence in the performance of their duties.

3. ETHICS

Each President's ethical behavior comes from the values, attitudes and knowledge that guide his or her judgments.

Every President has to make difficult decisions and complex choices every day, and those decisions and choices are to be made based on these eight guiding principles:

a. Accountability. Much like good people of every faith, you are answerable not only for your actions, but also for your omissions.

b. Fairness. You are required to treat all those for whom you are responsible fairly, equally and with self-control, tolerance and courtesy, without any consideration as to who among them is inclined to give you the most stuff or get you the most votes.

c. Integrity. You must always do the right thing, whether or not any "reward" is being proffered.
d. Leadership. You must fulfill all legal obligations of the Office of President, even when your instinct strongly suggests you do otherwise.
e. Selflessness. You are required to act in accordance with (i) the mandate from your citizens, (ii) in the public interest and (iii) in the interest of your nation regardless of any consequences to yourself.
f. Use of force. You will only use force as legally directed in accordance with your role and responsibilities, and only to the extent that it is necessary, proportionate and reasonable in the circumstances.
g. Fitness for work. You will ensure that you are physically and mentally fit to carry out your responsibilities. Note: Golf doesn't count.
h. Conduct. You will behave in a manner, whether on or off duty, which does not (i) bring discredit on your Office, your government, your nation or your citizens, or (ii) undermine public confidence in your Office or the government you have formed.

4. TRANSGRESSIONS, OFFENCES AND PUNISHMENT

While you can be forgiven almost any transgression from this code within the first hundred days of your Presidency, by which time you should have your act together and have, through your sage behavior signaled to those around you that you are now officially capable of assuming the Office of President, any lapse in behavior from that point forward is an offence.

For those of you who may be slow learners, you are permitted one teaching reprimand for a misdemeanor, which consists of a single, sharp "No!" barked loudly in your face.

Should you fail to heed that warning, the second level of permissible punishment is a swift, firm neck grab that forces you to instantly drop and roll onto your back.

Presidents do not get a "third chance". Any third misdemeanor is punishable by never again being taken seriously by the international community of Presidents, and by striking your name off the Master Membership List of the International Order of Presidents.

As harsh as this may sound, let's face it, if you can't get the message after two tries, there's probably a bit of reality T.V. star in you or some other cheerful, affectionate and sensitive breed of person. You, my friend, are merely an entertaining "personality" (known in the animal kingdom as a "pet").

For you, continuing to pretend to be a President is the equivalent of a person who plays "air guitar" calling himself a "musician".

You will have a wonderful life filled with hugs, kisses, applause, cuddles and treats. You may even write a book or get a T.V. show.

But you are not a President.

ABOUT THE AUTHOR

Gwynneth Mary Lovas is the author of *Canadian Military Law: Morale and Welfare Operations* (Carswell, 2013), *The Retirement Diaries®* (2016) and *How To Be A Good German Shepherd Dog: Self-Help For The Confused* (2017). She has been a member of the Law Society of Upper Canada since 1982, and spent the last twelve years of her legal career as a Department of Justice Senior Counsel providing advice to the Department of National Defence and the Canadian Forces. She currently works as a writer, lecturer and consultant, and owns and operates theretirementfairy.com, a web site dedicated to providing humorous retirement cards and gifts, and theretirementdiaries.com, a web site dedicated to humorous retirement stories based on her novels *The Retirement Diaries®* (2016) and *How To Be A Good German Shepherd Dog: Self-Help For The Confused* (2017).